BOOK OF
SHARKS

DR. DIANA PRINCE

AuthorHouse™
1663 Liberty Drive
Bloomington, IN 47403
www.authorhouse.com
Phone: 1 (800) 839-8640

Published by AuthorHouse 11/09/2018

ISBN: 978-1-5462-6789-8 (sc)
ISBN: 978-1-5462-6788-1 (e)
ISBN: 978-1-5462-6790-4 (hc)

Library of Congress Control Number: 2018913415

Print information available on the last page.

This book is printed on acid-free paper.

PHOTO CREDITS: All Photos are used with permission of Getty Images.

authorHOUSE®

Introduction

This book explores the amazing world of the shark. It is one of the world's most fascinating and feared creatures. Legends and myths about these unique animals have persisted since the beginning of time.

This book introduces young people to the vital role of sharks in the ecosystem, and their many types and variations.

Research and observations paint a picture of an endangered species being hunted, almost to extinction in some places, to simply use their fins as a food delicacy. This book explores both the facts and the myths about this unique creature.

Table of Contents

List of Photos

The World of Sharks

The many different species of sharks in the world share a unique feature called the "Ampullae of Lorenzini". This is an enhanced sensitivity by which they are able to detect living bodies in water. The ampullae are able to pick up the electro-magnetic field created by the movement of nearby bodies. The great white sharks have the most sensitive and keenest capability of detecting this electro-magnetic energy.

The fastest shark is the Mako Shark which can travel almost 100 miles an hour. Its smooth and slim-bodied build helps it to maneuver effortlessly in water.

There are many misconceptions about the threats sharks pose to humans. Generally, world-wide, attacks on humans cause fewer than 30 fatalities per year. However, there are some sharks which are known to attack humans more frequently. Those which pose the greatest threat are the Great White Shark, the Bull Sharks and the Tiger Sharks.

Despite the notoriety of the Great White Sharks as vicious aggressors, the most deadly sharks are, in fact, the Bull Sharks, who will often attack, even when they are not provoked. On the other hand, there are some sharks which will rarely attack humans. These include the Whale Shark, the Leopard Shark, the Angel Shark, the Nurse Shark and the Caribbean Reef Sharks.

In contrast, over a hundred million sharks are killed by humans each year, often for such delicacies as shark fin soup. This specialty is especially prized in Asiatic markets, where the rest of the shark, after having its fins cut off, is thrown back into the ocean to die. This is detrimental to the eco-system, and also a major threat to diminishing shark populations. Sharks will often attack other shark species. They are also sometimes pursued and killed by dolphins or Orca whales.

Observation

The shark is a remarkable animal. There have been some less than successful attempts to study them in captivity, primarily because such confinement has often produced negative effects on the sharks. Researchers have had their greatest success when they have studied sharks in their natural environment in the oceans of the world. Some of the earliest research began in the 1930's with the development of new underwater equipment.

Often diving teams will use special boats equipped with special monitoring equipment designed for the study of sharks. Also, specially constructed protective cages called "shark tanks" have made it possible for divers to make their observations of these unique animals at close range. These box-like enclosures have heavy protective steel bars. Often sharks will approach the rugged metal boxes out of curiosity, and bite the cage, mistaking it for food. Sharks do not have good vision, but they do have an excellent sense of smell.

Sharks can go into a frenzy when small fish or bait are dumped into their territory. It can be very dangerous if someone is not trained to deal with sharks and react quickly. This is a very serious activity. It is important for us to respect the environment in which these creatures make their home, and to study them with the least intrusion possible.

Despite precautions, there have been accidents recorded where sharks have been partially caught in the diving cages themselves. In some special shark "observation tanks", tourists have witnessed huge sharks thrashing in the water with such force that they have broken up the steel frames of the enclosures themselves. In some cases, the shark's head has penetrated the enclosures and caused bites or injuries to the observers inside. In other instances, sharks have damaged the diving cage door, and thrust the occupants out of the enclosure where they were immediately attacked.

Research

Jacques-Yves Cousteau was a member of the French Academy who was a co-inventor of the Aqua-Lung, and also helped develop some of the earliest scuba equipment, beginning in the 1930's. This was a great advancement for underwater exploration, and laid the groundwork for new scientific breakthroughs in shark research.

Today there are many scientists doing research on the habits of the shark. Scientists who study sharks are known as Marine Biologists. They take biological measurements, observe migratory habits, and track current shark populations to ensure stable numbers. They also advocate for legislation against senseless killing of sharks.

Some limited study is also conducted, for short periods of time, in laboratories and aquarium type enclosures where the sharks can be observed at close range in a research facility. These scientists will monitor temperature changes, and also conduct tests measuring activity and response times to different stimuli. However, because most sharks do not do well in captivity, researchers often find other ways to observe them, using researchers in dive tanks. Often sharks are briefly captured and "tagged" so that they can be monitored remotely. The tracking devices can relay information back to the research team, and the data can be used over time for future study and follow up.

One important object of study is the monitoring of sharks killed every year. A study at Dalhousie University in Halifax, Nova Scotia, determined that about 7 percent of every shark species is killed each year. Researcher, Boris Worm, determined that at least 100 million sharks are killed every year, a level not sustainable for shark populations. He reported these findings in *National Geographic* in 2013. Some centers for shark research today include programs at Duke University, the University of Hawaii, and Boston University.

Shark Size

THE LARGEST SHARKS

The Whale Shark

The largest fish in the world is the Whale Shark. The Guinness Records recorded the largest Whale Shark at over 40 feet in length, with a weight of 47,000 pounds.

The Great White Shark

The next largest species of shark, after the whale shark, is the Great White Shark. Although this shark is about three feet when born, it can reach a significant size. One of the largest sharks on record was a Great White Shark found in 1930 in the tidal waters of New Brunswick in Canada. It had entered the Saint John River at the Bay of Fundy. This shark measured 37 feet in length. In 1988, also in Canada, a 20-foot great white shark was caught in the Gulf of St. Lawrence.

In 1945, a large great white caught in Cuba, was given the nickname "Monster Shark". It was subdued by six fishermen in a relatively small boat. This shark measured 21 feet, and weighed 7,000 pounds.

The Tiger Shark

After the Great White Shark, the next largest shark is the Tiger Shark. Some of these have also been found in the 20-foot size range. They are typically slimmer in build than the great whites, and therefore weigh considerably less overall.

THE SMALLEST SHARKS

The very smallest shark is called the "Dwarf Lanternshark", which rarely exceeds a length of 9 inches. Another small species, the "Bonnet Head Shark" is about three feet in length.

Sharks Up Close

The thrill of observing sharks up close has been a driving factor for people to exhibit sharks in public places. These have had incredibly bad results. The first attempt occurred in 1955, at California's Marineland of the Pacific Aquatic Park. The relatively small 4-foot long shark required a one-million-gallon tank. The animal's lethargic behavior and failure to thrive resulted in its release shortly afterwards.

Such confinement resulted in a disorientation for these migratory animals, used to traversing long distances in the wild. They are biologically compelled to swim forward continuously, in order for their gills to be able to take in adequate oxygen. Also the saline balance on such a large tank must be constantly monitored.

Repeated attempts to exhibit Great White Sharks in public have been particularly difficult. It was noted that such confinement, even in a massive tank, caused them to collide with enclosure tank walls and sustain injuries. One conclusion was that their keen inner sense of direction and orientation were thwarted by the close confinement. Other theories suggested that crashing into glass walls was a result of stress imposed by confinement. The animals experienced repeated injuries and disorientation. Additionally, many sharks refused to eat dead fish, because their normal eating had required their own predatory hunting for live prey.

In 1984, a Great White Shark at the Monterey Bay Aquarium died after 11 days in captivity. Earlier, in 1981, a shark had died within two weeks because it refused to eat while in captivity. In 2004, Sea World had exhibited a Great White Shark in a 400,000-gallon tank. The animal experienced convulsions and died after 16 days in the tank. An incident in Japan in 2016 caused a similar shark death. In China in 2012, a 33-ton glass shark tank set up for visitors in a Shanghai shopping center burst open, injuring shoppers and killing the three sharks being exhibited.

Tiger Shark

Tiger Sharks get their name from the vertical black stripes characteristic of young sharks of this species. By adulthood, these markings have faded or disappeared altogether. They are a large species, ranging in size from ten feet to about 15 feet.

Adult Tiger Sharks range between 800 and 1200 pounds, but a few have been known to reach almost 1500 pounds. This species of shark is generally found in warm and tropical climates. Great numbers of Tiger Sharks are commonly found in such exotic locations as Melanesia, Polynesia and Micronesia.

If the water temperature decreases significantly, they will travel great distances, even thousands of miles, to find warmer water. They normally occupy deep water, but tend to feed in shallows, where the prey are more plentiful. They have a blunt-shaped nose, but their sense of smell is keen. This makes them skillful hunters. They are also able to detect prey from electrical impulses given off by such creatures as sea snakes and fish, even when the visibility is poor. Tiger Sharks will also prey on dolphins and even catch sea birds flying near the water surface.

Females only breed once every 3 years, due to the long pregnancies of Tiger Sharks, which average 15 months. These pregnancies produce as many as 80 offspring.

After Bull Sharks and Great White Sharks, the Tiger Sharks are the most dangerous to humans. Because they sometimes occupy harbors or shallow reefs, they are often in close proximity to humans, and after the great white shark, they have the next highest incidence of human fatalities from shark bites. Tiger Sharks have been known to live for fifty years.

Lemon Shark

Lemon Sharks are named for their characteristic yellow color. They prefer to congregate in surface waters where the water is warmer, and they are frequently found in bays and coral reefs. They are common in the coastal regions of both South America and North America.

Usually about 11 feet in length, and with an average weight of about 200 pounds, the Lemon Shark is considered a mid-size shark. Despite this, it is a powerful adversary. The Lemon Shark has powerful jaws and a solid, streamlined body built for swift swimming. It can be dangerous and aggressive.

The Lemon Shark will often target other sharks as prey in addition to the fish, crayfish, stingrays and squid which are its usual prey.

One interesting characteristic of the Lemon Shark is that the females return to the place where they were born in order to give birth there. This behavior is only known to occur among Lemon Sharks. The females breed about every two years. During gestation, an umbilical cord nourishes the developing offspring until they hatch. The females are able to store sperm over consecutive years, and therefore, the same male shark may be the father of consecutive litters from one year to the other.

At birth, the offspring are on their own. They take approximately six years to mature, during which time they inhabit the safer coastal shores, rather than entering into the deeper ocean. Lemon Sharks often live as long as thirty years.

While very few sharks are able to live well in captivity, the Lemon Shark is one of the few species that can thrive, even in captivity. They are the rare exception to be found and observed in aquariums. They are also part of "planned release programs" in which they are released into declining shark populations to ensure optimal shark numbers.

Oceanic White Tip Shark

The Oceanic White Tip Shark is known by a variety of names. It is also called a "Silvertip Shark" due to its distinct markings. It is also commonly known as a "Brown Milbert."

Because of its particularly large and rounded fins, it is sought after for the Asian shark fin soup market, which has drastically reduced its numbers. In recent surveys, the population of this Oceanic White Tip has declined by almost 80 percent over the last few decades, creating a significant threat to its survival.

Normally, these sharks travel alone, but they are sometimes spotted with other fish groups, or frequently swimming in the company of dolphins or even whales. This shark pursues food both day and night, unlike other sharks which often prefer evening hunting. Most grow to a full adult size of less than 10 feet, but they are sturdy and can easily reach about 220 pounds in weight. In this respect, it is usually the female who typically excels the male in size.

The Oceanic White Tip Sharks have 34 sharp teeth which can easily hold or cut their prey. They also have a wide-ranging appetite which includes sea turtles, squid, birds and stingrays. The Oceanic White Tip Sharks also eat several variations of fish including tuna, barracuda and marlin. Their embryos are nourished by an internal placenta, and the young develop in the uterus. Gestation lasts for a full year, with a normal birth of about a dozen offspring.

These sharks are hunted for food, for their hide and for oil. They have a reputation for being "opportunistic attackers." For instance, they have been known to attack survivors of shipwrecks, bathers congregated at resorts, or isolated divers. While they do not pursue human victims, they have taken advantage of isolated victims when found, such as survivors of ship accidents waiting in the water for rescue.

Great White Shark

Great White Sharks are common in coastal waters, preferring regions with warmer water temperatures such as those in South Africa, South America, California and the Baja Peninsula. In ocean waters, these sharks can travel as fast as 35 miles per hour. They can also be found at great depths as deep as 4,000 feet.

They are the most deadly shark with respect to human fatalities than any other shark species. Normally, however, they eat smaller sharks, dolphins, whales, seals and tuna. Even small creatures such as birds and turtles are eaten. A Great White Shark can ingest over 25 pounds of food in one bite.

Great White Sharks are known to execute what is referred to as a "breach", which is a sudden, quick jump out of the water, usually to surprise their prey. On some occasions, they will leap eight feet or more above the water surface. Great White Sharks and Orca whales will sometime compete, usually for food in an area. Alone or in groups, they are formidable enemies who kill each other to gain control of a region.

Females are dominant over males in this species. Also, size is a determinant of power within a group. Great White Sharks have been known to bite one another. Whether this relates to dominance, or protecting their territory, is not known. In the social groups which travel together, there is an established "alpha" member which presides over the other group members.

The gestation period is almost a year, and the young are an average length of 3 feet at birth, usually in late spring. Males take 26 years to reach maturity, before they are able to reproduce. Females reach maturity and reproductive age at about 35 years of age. These long gestation and maturity times are significant factors in the decreasing numbers of the Great White Shark population. Their average life span is 70 years.

Blue Shark

The Blue Shark is one of the most widely distributed shark species in the world. There is almost no region in the world in which this species is not found. However, unlike other species which prefer warm coastal regions, blue sharks also thrive in cold water at great depths. They will often frequent depths of water well below 1,000 feet.

Unlike most species which return to particular locations year after year, Blue Sharks are often on the move for new hunting or mating territories. If necessary, they will travel thousands of miles during the mating season. Over 100 offspring can be produced by a single Blue Shark during one birthing period. It can take a year for the gestation of offspring, and it can take five years for the newborns to reach adulthood.

This particular species is believed to be one of the fastest swimmers among the sharks, reaching speeds in excess of 55 miles per hour in some instances.

Fish and squid are the primary foods of the Blue Shark. The Blue Sharks can reach a weight of over 500 pounds, and they average about ten feet in length.

The Blue Sharks, themselves, are the prey of sea lions. In addition, they are also targeted by other larger sharks such as the Great White Shark. But their greatest predators are humans, who hunt the animal for their distinctive skins.

Blue Sharks are rarely a threat to humans. Many of the incidents in which humans were bitten are believed to have occurred when humans were mistaken for other prey.

Leopard Shark

Leopard Sharks are commonly found along the Pacific Coast from Washington State to the tip of Mexico. The largest coming together of Leopard Sharks takes place every year off La Jolla Shores in San Diego, California. This event usually occurs in late August, when the greatest numbers of Leopard Sharks in the world congregate here.

These Leopard Sharks who congregate at La Jolla Shores are almost exclusively female, and many are pregnant. The waters here are shallow and warm, and ideal for gestation of the Leopard Sharks. At that time, the average temperatures in the water are in the mid-seventies Fahrenheit.

The pregnancy of the Leopard Shark lasts ten months. Each mother will produce up to 20 offspring. The newborn sharks do not reach maturity for ten years.

The local Birch Aquarium and Research Center organizes tours, in which people can observe these creatures up close. They can scuba dive or swim with the sharks. They are non-threatening to humans. Although the Leopard Sharks are meat eaters, they are not known to have attacked humans.

Their black and tan spots, which resemble the spots of leopards, are so individualized that sharks can be recognized by their unique markings.

These sharks consume crabs, squid, shrimp and fish. They have about 80 teeth, which are quite small and sharp, and well-equipped to eat small crustaceans.

Most adult Leopard Sharks range from 3 to 5 feet, but some have been known to reach much greater lengths. Their life expectancy is believed to be about 25 years.

Grey Reef Shark

The Grey Reef Sharks prefer the shallow water usually found in the vicinity of coral reefs. They inhabit the Pacific coastal waters in Indonesia, but have also been sighted off the coast of South Africa, and the coastal waters off South America near Chile. They are also commonly found in the Indian Ocean, the Red Sea and even Hawaii.

Grey Reef Sharks produce a small number of offspring at one time. Their gestation period is well over a year, with births occurring only every other year. They do not reach reproductive maturity until a much later age than most other sharks, and therefore their reproductive rates are much lower than other species. This means that they are very vulnerable in terms of their numbers. There are usually only four or fewer offspring in each litter.

The Grey Reef Shark usually reaches a moderate size of only 6 or 7 feet, and usually weighs about 40 pounds. This species hunts in groups, usually at night. Grey Reef Sharks can be aggressive to other predators and also to humans. When threatened, they will employ a zig-zag swimming pattern as a warning.

Their powerful jaws have about 28 teeth. Although they primarily range in water that is only 300 feet deep, they will sometimes dive to a depth as deep as 3,500 feet. Mostly they forage for food in the corals and shallow waters. Their main prey are octopus, squid, crabs and lobsters. They are known for their particularly keen sense of smell.

Normally they travel in groups of 30 to 40 individuals. Their normal life span in the wild is about 26 years.

Whale Shark

The Whale Shark is the largest fish in the world. Whale Sharks are no relation to whales who are four times longer, and weigh significantly more. However, whales are not fish at all, but mammals like dolphins.

The Whale Shark has a flat wide head, and a large mouth. These sharks have been known to reach 45 feet in length and can weigh over 20,000 pounds. They are not fast swimmers, and rarely travel more than 10 miles per hour. They are very rarely aggressive.

Whale Sharks subsist on plankton, shrimp, fish, squid and other small microorganisms which they ingest through their open mouth while swimming through the water. This type of food assimilation is called "filter feeding". An intriguing feature is that the Whale Shark has nearly 3,000 very small teeth in successive rows which catch and hold the ingested prey. In a 24-hour period, they can ingest up to 40 pounds of plankton. The Whale Shark is able to get oxygen from water as it breathes in through its gills. It has five sets of gills to accomplish this.

Each year in spring, hundreds of Whale Sharks migrate to the west coast of Australia in large numbers.

At birth the offspring are usually less than 2 feet long. A unique feature of the female Whale Shark is that she can carry several hundred eggs, often up to 300 eggs at one time. However, the offspring do not mature at the same time. Therefore, she can periodically give birth while retaining many of the eggs for later birth. Once born, it takes an individual Whale Shark over 20 years to reach maturity.

Whale Sharks are believed to live approximately 100 years.

Hammerhead Shark

The Hammerhead Shark is found in warm coastal waters worldwide. They are easily identifiable by their flat heads which are elongated laterally, and resemble the shape of a hammer. These heads can be used to catch and subdue prey.

The Hammerhead Sharks are generally 12 feet long, and they average about 600 pounds. They have rarely been known to reach over 20 feet in length. Their mouths are relatively smaller than most other sharks. Hammerheads are very rarely known to attack humans. There have been rare injuries to humans, but no reported deaths.

The Hammerhead Shark is believed to have evolved more recently than other sharks. While sharks were known to exist 400 million years ago, the evolution of this particular species appears to have occurred more recently in the geological period about 25 million years ago. Altogether, there are nine different types of Hammerhead Sharks. Within the species, there are variations such as the "Scalloped Hammerheads", the "Bonnet Heads" and the "Wingheads".

The white belly of the Hammerhead Shark camouflages it when it is underwater, and allows it to attack victims by surprise. Hammerhead Sharks will often subsist on squid or fish. They have even been known to attack and eat other Hammerhead Sharks, and have even been known to eat their offspring.

The mating ritual begins when the male shark initiates breeding by biting the female. The mating results in approximately a dozen offspring. In the unusual case of the "Bonnet Head Shark", the female is able to produce offspring without a male. This is the only known type of shark able to do this. The Hammerhead Sharks have been widely killed for their fins which are prized as food.

Caribbean Reef Shark

The Caribbean Reef Sharks live in the tropical waters of the West Atlantic. They are also found as far north as Florida, and as far south as Brazil. These sharks occupy the Caribbean and the Bahamas, where they live among the coral reefs. Also, in Bermuda and the Gulf of Mexico, they thrive in the shallow warm coastal waters.

The nose, or snout, of the Caribbean Reef Shark is shorter and more rounded than in most other shark species. Unlike other sharks, they will often rest unobtrusively on the floor of the ocean, or hover inside caves, giving the appearance that they are sleeping. These sharks reach an average of nine feet in length.

Pregnancy occurs on alternating years, and the gestation period is an entire year. There are only about 6 offspring in each litter, which are far fewer than most other shark species which produce hundreds of offspring. The offspring of the Caribbean Reef Shark are often the prey of larger sharks, especially the Tiger Shark.

The Caribbean Reef Shark can be dangerous and aggressive, although their attacks on humans are rarely fatal. They are hunted for their leather, liver oil, meat, and the unlawful marketing in shark fins.

In the Bahamas, there is a thriving business in shark viewing, during which hundreds gather to witness the frenzied feeding of these sharks responding to bait thrown into their midst.

The diminishing coral reefs are currently robbing more and more of the Caribbean Reef Sharks of their natural habitats. Also excessive fishing, particularly in Cuba and Mexico, has resulted in a marked decrease in this shark population. The current life span of the Caribbean Reef Shark is about twenty years.

Printed in the United States
By Bookmasters